99

A Pillar Box Red Publication

ISBN 978-1-907823-06-0

we love you...

TAKE THAT

An Unauthorised 2011 Annual

Written by Sarah Milne

Designed by Chris Dalrymple

CONTENTS

we love you...

TAKE THAT

because...

You are committed to charity work, and not afraid of getting stuck in to help others.

Even The Queen wants you to come to her birthday party!

Take That tours are always amazing spectacles – you really know how to put on a show.

You all have a sense of humour.

You have been together through thick and thin.

You are grateful for the support of your fans, both old and new.

You never forget where you've come from.

You write simply fantastic pop songs.

You have developed your own sense of style and know how to show off your best bits!

History: The Early Days

After seeing the success of US boy band, New Kids on the Block, music manager Nigel Martin-Smith decided that he wanted to create a similar group in the UK.

He set up auditions for the band in Manchester and the Northwest. Nigel had already met Gary Barlow through a friend who was an agent, and was impressed with Gary's song-writing skills. Howard managed to get time off his work at a car-spraying plant to successfully audition, and suggested Jason would be a good member too. Robbie and Mark first met at their audition.

The band first appeared on TV show The Hitman and Her in 1990, and first single Do What U Like was released in 1991, reaching number 82 in the UK charts. The next year, their single It Only Takes a Minute Girl reached number seven in the charts and put Take That on the road to stardom.

The next four singles were successes too, all getting into the Top Twenty, but in 1993, Pray became their first UK number one - and there were another three to follow! 1994 and 1995 seemed to be going well for the boys with them notching up lots of hits and planning to tour America.

But then, in July 1995, Robbie announced he was leaving Take That. The remaining four announced they would be carrying on.

Take That continued as a foursome for the rest of the year but announced in 1996 (on Robbie's 22nd birthday) that they would be splitting up. Fans were devastated, and helplines were set up to help them deal with the split. Take That's final performance was in Amsterdam in April 1996.

We all thought that was the end of the best boy band ever. Until ten years later…

History: Rise to Fame

Take That fans thought they had seen the last of the boys performing as a group, though many had successful solo careers. Then, in November 2005, a new compilation album of the band's hit singles was released. The same month, the four boys (minus Robbie) got together for an ITV documentary about the band, and announced that they would be touring in 2006.

The Ultimate Tour was only supposed to run to 11 dates, but, after tickets sold out in only half an hour, this was extended to 32 shows across the UK and Ireland. It would be an understatement to say that this tour was a success...

In May 2006, Take That signed a new record contract, rumoured to be worth £3million! The new album, Beautiful World, entered the charts at number one, and has since gone eight times platinum. Single Patience was released in November that year and, again, went straight in at number one.

2007 saw the boys perform at the BRIT Awards, where Patience won the award for Best British Single, and the Beautiful World Tour, which saw them take in the New Year at London's O_2 Arena.

In 2008, Take That won BRIT awards for Best Live Act and Best British Single for Shine. Greatest Day was the first single from The Circus album and went straight in at number one (can you spot a trend here?). The Circus broke all records before it was even released, to become the most preordered album of all time.

Summer 2009, and the boys were back on the road again, with The Circus Live Tour, which was one of the most amazing live shows the fans had ever seen - complete with a massive moving elephant in the middle of the stage - the audience certainly got more than they bargained for!

Spot the Difference

Can you spot all 7 differences in the pictures below?

Answers on page 60

Name: Mark Owen

Date of Birth: 27th January 1972

Birthplace: Oldham, Manchester

Star Sign: Aquarius

When the band first started, Mark was always seen as the 'cute' one, and often won the title of Most Fanciable Male at the annual Smash Hits awards.

At school Mark was more interested in football than music, and in the early Take That days he never wrote his own songs. The first time he sang lead was on the hit Babe, released in December 1993.

Since Take That reformed, Mark has taken a much bigger role in both songwriting and in vocal performance.

Mark is married to actress Emma Ferguson and they have two gorgeous children, Elwood and Willow.

In 2002, Mark won the second series of celebrity Big Brother, and was in floods of tears when Davina announced his name as the winner.

Wordsearch

Can you find all the words hidden in the grid below?
Remember, they could be in any direction!

```
T D L R O W E H T E L U R L M
E E H M X P N L D W L N R A K
G E F O M C J T R O K M N Q M
R N Z R M G Q J L G N C L M R
O N D A S U C R I C H A T X O
F I F N Y R Y F W E M S L L W
R N Z G R N F T S D M V L D L
E E L E Q X Y T R A B E Q J V
V R J R Z P E L I G V W N D T
E D R Y E R K L T O M O W N N
N L P P Y N L Y N T X L L H Q
V I P N T I I R W F D R M Z L
Y H Z F W F O H V N M A Y F L
F C P L R V C Y S X Z B J R C
O W E N I P V M G Y G H J M X
```

Barlow	Circus
Williams	Shine
Owen	Children in Need
Donald	Rule the World
Orange	Ivor Novello
Manchester	Never Forget

Solution on page 60

Spotlight on Gary

Name: Gary Barlow

Date of Birth: 20th January 1971

Birthplace: Frodsham, Cheshire

Star Sign: Capricorn

Gary first decided he wanted to work in music when he heard 80s legends Depeche Mode perform their classic hit I Just Can't Get Enough on Top of the Pops in 1980. He decided then that he wanted a keyboard for Christmas, and the rest is history. Gary taught himself how to play.

Gary then went on to reach the semi-finals in a TV talent show looking for A Song for Christmas, and he was invited to London to record his track. This early success encouraged Gary to start performing at clubs in the Northwest of England.

Gary met his wife Dawn in 1995, when she was a backing dancer on the Take That Nobody Else tour. They married in 2000, and have three children, Daniel, Emily and Daisy. Family has always been the most important aspect of Gary's life.

Because of his music industry connections and commitment to charity work, Gary has been asked by Her Majesty the Queen to help organise her 85th birthday celebrations in 2012. It should be quite a knees-up!

After walking up Africa's Mount Kilimanjaro for Comic Relief in 2009, Gary is now planning a charity walk to the North Pole and back for BBC Sport Relief.

As well as a fantastic performer and all round good guy, Gary is a well-respected and successful songwriter, and in addition to his solo and Take That work, has written hit songs for many other artists, including Will Young and Charlotte Church.

Gary has been awarded the Ivor Novello award five times, and has also been voted the greatest British songwriter of all time - ahead of Paul McCartney from the Beatles!

Discography

Never let it be said that that band are lazy - so far they have released eight albums and 24 singles - phew! Most of those were sure fire hits, as the discography below shows.

Albums (peak chart positions and sales certifications are for UK charts)

1992: Take That and Party. Number 2. Double Platinum

1993: Everything Changes. Number 1. Quadruple Platinum

1995: Nobody Else. Number 1. Double Platinum

1996: Greatest Hits. Number 1. Triple Platinum

2002: Forever... Greatest Hits. Number 123

2005: Never Forget: The Ultimate Collection. Number 2. Triple Platinum

2006: Beautiful World. Number 1. Eight-times Platinum

2006: The Platinum Collection. Number 127

2008: The Circus. Number 1. Seven-times Platinum

2009: The Greatest Day - Take That Present: The Circus Live. Number 3. Live Album

Singles

1991: Do What U Like. Number 82

1991: Promises. Number 38

1992: Once You've Tasted Love. Number 47

1992: It Only Takes A Minute. Number 7

1992: I Found Heaven. Number 15

1992: A Million Love Songs. Number 7

1992: Could It Be Magic. Number 3. Silver

1993: Why Can't I Wake Up With You. Number 2. Silver

1993: Pray. Number 1. Gold

1993: Relight My Fire (with Lulu). Number 1. Silver

1993: Babe. Number 1. Platinum

1994: Everything Changes. Number 1. Silver

1994: Love Ain't Here Anymore. Number 3. Silver

1994: Sure. Number 1. Silver

1995: Back For Good. Number 1. Platinum

1995: Never Forget. Number 1. Gold

1996: How Deep Is Your Love. Number 1. Platinum

2006: Patience. Number 1. Gold

2007: Shine. Number 1. Silver

2007: I'd Wait For Life. Number 17

2007: Rule The World. Number 2. Gold

2008: Greatest Day. Number 1. Silver

2009: Up All Night. Number 14

2009: The Garden. Number 97

2009: Said It All. Number 9

Live on Stage

Aww - Mark and Robbie share a hug as Robbie joins the band on stage at the BBC Children in Need Rocks concert at the Albert Hall.

Gary and Robbie are joined on stage by Lily Allen for a special performance at the BBC Children in Need Rocks concert at the Albert Hall.

The band soak up the atmosphere on stage at Wembley Arena.

In 2006, the reformed four-piece kick off their reunion tour at the Metro Radio Arena in Newcastle.

International stars, performing at the 'Festival di Sanremo' Italian song contest.

Getting up close and personal at the Odyssey Arena, Belfast.

Performing at the Brit Awards 2007, shortly after reforming.

Emotional times at the Concert for Diana.

An energetic performance at Birmingham's NEC.

Live at the O₂ Arena.

The MTV Music Video Awards Show in Liverpool brought a huge audience.

Coming home – on stage at the MEN Arena in Manchester.

Flying high at the Brit Awards 2009.

Crossword

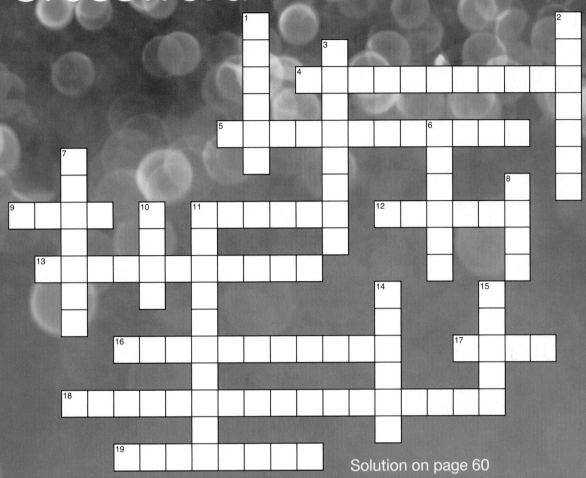

Solution on page 60

ACROSS

4   This fruity member of the band has a twin called Justin (5, 6)

5   Howard and Jason met while doing this (12)

9   60s singer, duetted with the band on Relight my Fire (4)

11 Gary Barlow's first autobiography (2, 4)

12 _____ Aid - the football charity the band like to support (6)

13 Gary walked up here for Comic Relief (11)

16 "We've come so far" - opening lyrics from which number one? (5, 6)

17 Do What U _____ - the boys' first release (4)

18 This album was nominated for the mercury Music Prize in 1994 (10, 7)

19 Rule The World was written for this film (8)

DOWN

1   Jason and which other band member do people often get confused (6)

2   The boys did a bit of modelling work for high street store, Marks & _____ (7)

3   Could one of the cutest members of the band really be 'MEAN WORK' (anagram) (4, 4)

6   This 2009 Tour was a huge success (6)

7   40 _____ - the number of records the band has sold since getting back together (7)

8   Take That's first number one hit - was it divine intervention? (4)

10 "Feels like coming _____" – Robbie said this about rejoining the band (4)

11 City in the Northwest where the band first formed (10)

14 This TV show is where Take That made their debut performance. The _____ And Her (6)

15 The band has won seven of these awards (so far) (5)

Spotlight on Robbie

Name: Robert Peter Williams

Date of Birth: 13th February 1974

Birthplace: Stoke-on-Trent, Staffordshire

Star Sign: Aquarius

In 2010, Robbie celebrates 20 years in the music industry. Can you believe he was only 16 when he first joined Take That?

Robbie went solo in 1995, but announced in mid-2010 that he had rejoined the group for the original line-up's new album, released later that year.

Robbie loves football, and is a keen supporter of his hometown club, Port Vale FC - there's even a restaurant at the club named after him!

If you like to sing along with Robbie, a new game for the Nintendo Wii, We Sing Robbie Williams, was released in Autumn 2010.

Robbie has made it into the Guinness Book of Records four times!

- Most albums to reach number one in the UK chart by a British solo male artist.

- Most BRIT awards won by an individual - 14 in total!

- Most entries at number one made consecutively on the UK album chart by a solo artist - five in a row.

- Most tour tickets sold in a day (concerts) - a total of 1.6million tickets, valued at £80million were sold in the first 24 hours for Robbie Williams' 2006 World Tour.

In February 2010, Robbie received the award for Outstanding Contribution To British Music at the BRIT Awards.

Robbie loves UFOs and claims to have seen three: one when he was a little boy and two in America.

"It feels like coming home" - Robbie's thoughts on rejoining Take That. Our feelings exactly!

Awards

As well as selling millions of singles, and having armies of loyal fans, Take That have also been recognised by the music industry, and have been lucky enough to win lots of awards. Hope there's still some room on their mantelpieces – there are sure to be plenty of awards still to come!

2009: GQ Men Of The Year Awards for Best Band.

2009: Q Award for Best Live Act (nominated).

2009: BRIT Award for Best British Group (nominated).

2008: Shine - Ivor Novello Award for PRS Most Performed Work.

2008: Sony Ericsson Tour Of The Year Award for Take That Arena Tour.

2008: Shine - BRIT Award for Best British Single.

2008: BRIT Award for Best British Live Act.

2008: Beautiful World - BRIT Award for Best British Album (nominated).

2008: BRIT Award for Best British Group (nominated).

2007: Patience BRIT Award for Best British Single.

2006: Q Idol Award.

1996: Back for Good - BRIT Award for Best British Single.

1995: MTV Europe Music Awards for Best Live Act.

1994: Pray - BRIT Award for Best British Single.

1994: Pray - BRIT Award for Best British Video.

1994: MTV Europe Music Awards for Best Group.

1993: Could it be Magic - BRIT Award for Best British Single.

Mega Quiz

1. What number in the UK charts did Take That's first single Do What U Like reach?
2. What was the band's first UK single and when did it top the charts?
3. Which American boy band inspired original manager Nigel Martin Smith to set up Take That in the first place?
4. What is the name of the musical based around the band's Greatest Hits?
5. Which film used Rule the World as its theme tune?
6. Which Thatter won Celebrity Big Brother in 2002?
7. What did Gary Barlow do for Comic Relief in 2009?
8. When Howard DJs, what name is he known by?
9. Which member of the band has a twin brother?
10. Which band member claims to have seen three UFOs?
11. What date did Take That split up, and why was it also significant?
12. Which 60s singing legend sang with the band on the hit Relight My Fire?
13. Could It Be Magic was originally a hit for which singer in the 1970s?
14. Where did the Circus Live tour start?
15. Which high street store has the band modelled suits for?
16. In what year did the band win the Q magazine Idol Award?
17. How did Robbie describe rejoining the band in 2010?
18. Which American girl group supported the band in Dublin during the Ultimate Tour?
19. Which city was the band formed in?
20. How many singles have the band sold since reforming in 2005?

Answers on page 61

Spotlight on Jason

Name: Jason Thomas Orange

Date of Birth: 10th July 1970

Birthplace: Manchester

Star Sign: Cancer

Jason left school with no qualifications and became an apprentice painter and decorator.

Jason's first TV experience was showing off his break-dancing skills on 80s show The Hitman and Her.

He met Howard while break-dancing in Manchester.

After Take That split up in 1996, Jason was the only member of the group not to launch a solo singing career, and instead went to New York to study acting. He appeared in a Channel 4 thriller as a DJ, as well as acting on stage. Jason also travelled the world and went to college, studying psychology, biology, history and sociology.

Jason performed lead vocals live for the first time in 2007, on the song Wooden Boat, which was the opening song of the Beautiful World Tour.

Jason first picked up a guitar while the group were recording Babe, and now often plays live on stage.

37

Take That Gossip

There's probably not much that you don't know already about your fav band, but here are a few snippets you might not have heard before…

80s children's TV star Timmy Mallett was a guest at Gary Barlow's 10th anniversary party. Why? Because Gary's wife Dawn appeared in the video for his number one single, Itsy Bitsy Teeny Weenie Yellow Polka Dot Bikini in 1990.

When the group disbanded, Gary's wax model at Madame Tussauds was melted down to make way for Britney Spears!

When Gary, Mark and Robbie first got together they were called The Cutest Rush. Then when Howard and Jason joined, they were Kick It, then Take That and Party, then finally Take That.

The band's final name came from a magazine which featured Madonna and read 'Madonna: Take that and party'.

Spotlight on Howard

Name: Howard Donald

Date of Birth: 28th April 1968

Birthplace: Manchester

Star Sign: Taurus

Howard has two daughters, Grace and Lola.

Howard's mum was a singer and his dad a dance teacher, so it seems inevitable that he wanted to perform himself.

Howard's childhood dream was to be a pilot, but he ended up starting an apprenticeship as a car sprayer when he left school.

Break-dancing was his real passion, and that's where he first met Jason.

When Take That were on their break, Howard became, and still is, a very popular House DJ and has DJd all over the world. He performs under the name of DJ HD.

As a DJ, Howard has a huge following in Germany.

After some particularly energetic moves on stage in 2007, Howard suffered a collapsed lung, and was kept in hospital for two days.

On the song Mancunian Way, from the Beautiful World album, as well as Howard singing lead vocals, his daughter Grace can be heard singing at the end of the track.

Collaborations

Even from the early days of the band, Take That have been keen to work with other artists in exciting and sometimes unexpected collaborations.

Rumoured collaborations that have never quite happened include Take That and 80s legends Spandau Ballet. In 2008, Gary mentioned that it would be good to work with Girls Aloud. Fellow boy-turned-man-band Boyzone were also reported to be interested in working with Take That.

Take That

Lulu - Relight My Fire

Beverley Knight - Relight My Fire (Live on the Ultimate Tour)

Lily Allen - onstage at Children in Need Rocks

Robbie

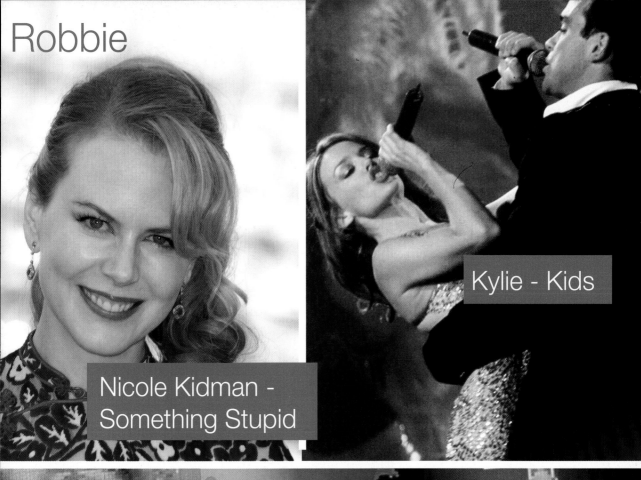

Nicole Kidman - Something Stupid

Kylie - Kids

Pet Shop Boys - She's Madonna

Neil Tennant (Pet Shop Boys) and Neil Hannon (Divine Comedy) - No Regrets

Gary Barlow - Shame

Lily Allen - Bongo Bong and Je Ne T'Aime Plus

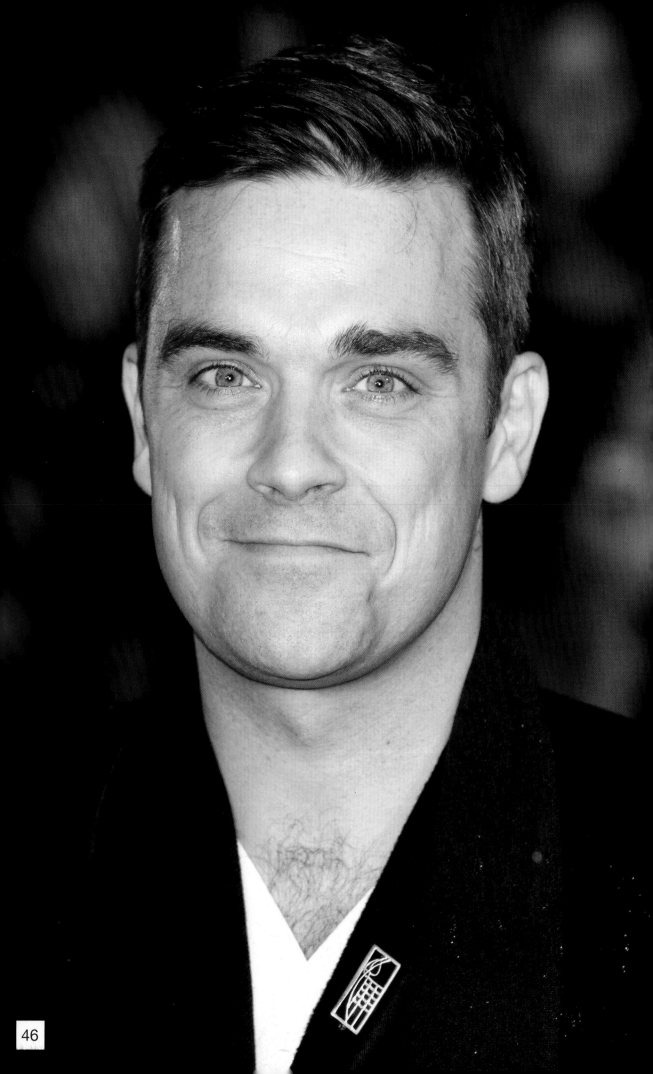

Spot the Difference

There are 7 changes between the two pictures below – can you spot them all?

Answers on page 61

Take That Facts & Figures

1990 - Take That make their first TV appearance.

1993 - First number one, Pray, released.

1995 - Robbie leaves.

2005 - The band reform.

25 million - the number of records the band sold between 1991 and 1996.

2010 - Robbie rejoins for new album.

40 million (and counting) - the number of records the band has sold since reforming in 2005.

7 – The number of BRIT awards won so far.

24 singles released

8 albums

16 number one records (albums and singles)

6 tours, 3 since they reformed. Next tour due in 2011, with Robbie back in the fold.

650,000 - The number of tickets sold for The Circus Live Tour in just four and a half hours.

133,000 - The number of copies The Circus album sold on the first day of release.

Back for Good

This time round, are Take That really back for good? We all hope so.

In June 2010, Robbie Williams announced that his new single, Shame, was co-written and co-performed with Gary Barlow.

There were lots of rumours that Robbie would rejoin the band and he was even spotted with the rest of the boys in New York. Then on July 15th 2010, came the announcement everyone was waiting for:

"Following months of speculation, Gary Barlow, Howard Donald, Jason Orange, Mark Owen and Robbie Williams confirmed today that they have been recording a new studio album as a five piece, which they will release in November of this year. It is the first time they've recorded a full album together since the release of their number one album Nobody Else, back in 1995."

This is what some of the boys themselves had to say about it:

“ *Getting the five of us to be in a room together, although always a dream, never actually seemed like becoming a reality. Now the reality of the five of us making a record together feels like a dream. It's been an absolute delight spending time with Rob again. But I'm still a better footballer.* **”**

Mark Owen

“ *I get embarrassingly excited when the five of us are in a room. It feels like coming home.* **”**

Robbie Williams

“ *Flippin' brilliant, absolutely brilliant. I'm over the moon that Robbie's back with us, however long it lasts. I just want to enjoy our time with him. Life is beautifully strange sometimes.* **”**

Jason Orange

The first single the band will release as a reformed five piece is to be called The Flood, and the boys were spotted in a rowing boat filming the video. We just can't wait!

51

Take That Fashion

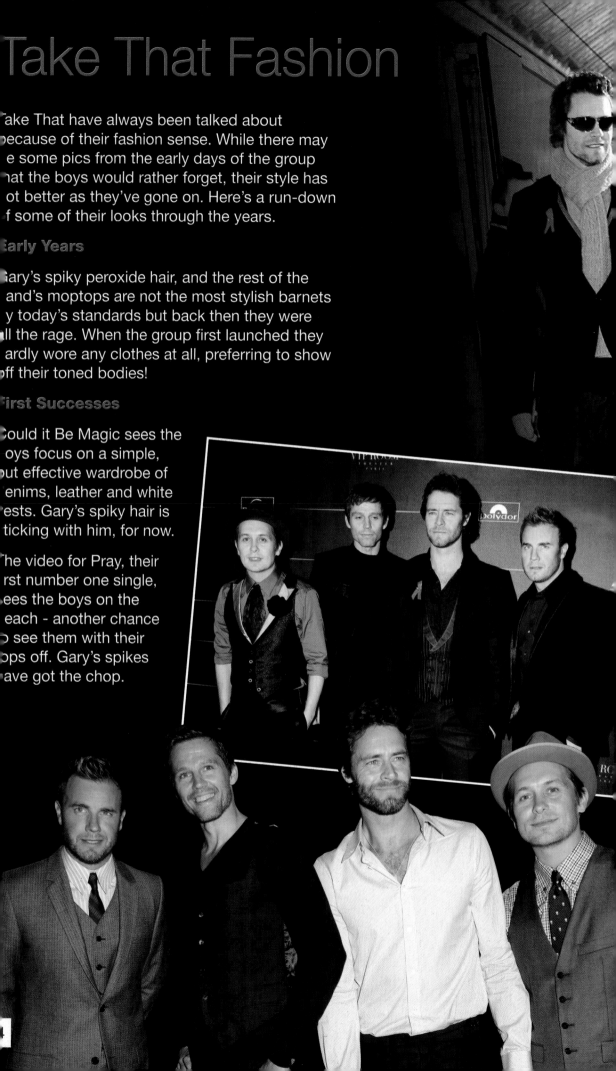

Take That have always been talked about because of their fashion sense. While there may be some pics from the early days of the group that the boys would rather forget, their style has got better as they've gone on. Here's a run-down of some of their looks through the years.

Early Years

Gary's spiky peroxide hair, and the rest of the band's moptops are not the most stylish barnets by today's standards but back then they were all the rage. When the group first launched they hardly wore any clothes at all, preferring to show off their toned bodies!

First Successes

Could it Be Magic sees the boys focus on a simple, but effective wardrobe of denims, leather and white vests. Gary's spiky hair is sticking with him, for now.

The video for Pray, their first number one single, sees the boys on the beach - another chance to see them with their tops off. Gary's spikes have got the chop.

Back for Good - Robbie's last single with the band, and the boys have all started to develop their own individual style. Howard has dreadlocks, Robbie's hair is shaved, Gary is looking slick while Mark and Jason are rocking more shaggy styles.

The New Era

The boys relaunch with a much more mature look. Smart tailoring, chunky knitwear and great haircuts make for a great look. The Shine video sees the boys dress up in

their finest for a slick look - and Howard's dreads have gone.

In 2008, the boys modelled for Marks and Spencer, appearing in their Christmas advert alongside Myleene Klass, model Lily Cole and Twiggy.

On Stage

The live tours offer the boys a real chance to show off their creativity, and do a little dressing up. Gangsters, clowns and soldiers - they've tried all these looks, with lots of success.

he boys have always been keen
help others that are less lucky
an themselves. From wounded
oldiers to children in poverty, Take
nat certainly do their bit in raising
wareness and money, to benefit
eir favourite charities. Here's a
uick look at some of the projects
ey've been involved in.

August 2010, it was announced
nat Robbie Williams would be
eadlining at the Heroes Concert,
eld in aid of Help the Heroes, a
narity which provides support for
oldiers injured in conflicts.

2009, Gary led a team of
elebrities on a climb up Mount
ilimanjaro, for Comic Relief. The
ountain is Africa's highest, at 5893
etres above sea-level. The team
ised a whopping £3.5 million for
e charity.

ary is now rumoured to be planning
trek to the North Pole in 2012 to
aise money for BBC Sport Relief.
could take a week of trekking
hrough the Arctic to reach the pole.

The band sang on Everybody Hurts, the REM cover put together by Simon Cowell in early 2010 to raise money for the victims of the devastating earthquakes in Haiti.

In 2009, Gary also organised Children in Need Rocks at the Royal Albert Hall, when Robbie joined the band on stage for the first time since the split. The band also performed with Lily Allen on stage. The event raised over £2million.

In 2008, the band performed their new single Greatest Day on BBC's Children in Need. The boys then donated £250,000, which came from their Marks & Spencer modelling jobs, to the fund.

At the beginning of May 2010, it was announced that Her Majesty The Queen has asked Gary Barlow to organise her 85th birthday and her Diamond Jubilee celebrations in 2012.

Robbie, along with friend Jonathan Wilkes set up Soccer Aid, with the first match in 2006. It raises money for UNICEF UK.

A to Z of Take That

A: Awards - Take That have won many over their career so far, and there's plenty more to come!

B: Birthday Celebrations - Gary has been asked by the Queen to help organise her 85th birthday party!

C: The Circus. Second album released after reforming. It went platinum after 4 days on sale.

D: DJ HD - Howard's name when he performs as a DJ.

E: Everything Changes - the band's fourth single in a row to go to number one in the UK charts.

F: Fans – Take That fans have been loyal from the early days to now, with mums and daughters going to concerts together.

G: Generous - the boys devote a lot of time to charity work, with Gary even planning a charity walk to the North Pole. Brrr....

H: The Hitman and Her. Take That's very first TV appearance.

I: Ivor Novello Awards. Prestigious song-writing awards which Take That won for Shine in 2008.

J: July 2010 - the month that Take That announced Robbie would be returning to the band.

K: Knight, Beverley. The gorgeous soul singer Beverley Knight joined the boys on stage in 2006.

L: Lulu. Legendary singer who featured on Relight My Fire.

M: Manchester, where it all began in 1991.

N: Never Forget. One of the band's last singles before splitting in 1996, and also the title of one of their compilation albums.

O: On Tour - the original line-up will be touring in 2011 - yippee!

P: Pray - Take That's first ever Number 1 hit. The lovely Mark sang lead vocals too.

Q: Q Idol Award - the band won this in 2006.

R: Robbie Williams rejoins! The world rejoices!

S: Stardust - the film features Rule The World as it's theme tune.

T: Twin - Jason has a twin brother, Justin. Jason is the oldest twin.

U: Ultimate Tour - first live gigs since reforming.

V: Videos - the boys always make eye-catching videos to promote the singles.

W: Willow - Mark's daughter has the cutest name. Son's name Elwood is pretty sweet too!

X: X Factor. The band appeared on the show at the end of 2008, when the finalists performed some of Take That's greatest hits.

Y: 20 Years - the band first started in 1990, over 20 years ago - can you believe it?

Z: Zeds - the boys are going to be so busy over the next few years, they'd be wise to get some sleep while they can.

Quiz Answers

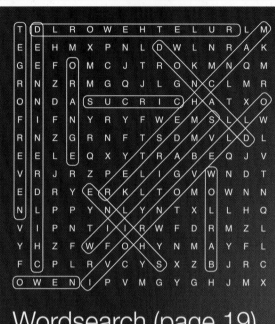

Wordsearch (page 19)

Crossword (page 27)

Spot the Difference (page 15)

Mega Quiz (page 34)

1 82 (it does have a rather saucy video though!)

2 Pray in 1993

3 New Kids on the Block (also recently reformed, but not yet as successfully as Take That)

4 Never Forget

5 Stardust

6 Mark Owen

7 Climb Mount Kilimanjaro

8 DJ HD

9 Jason

10 Robbie

11 13th February 1996 (also Robbie's 22nd birthday)

12 Lulu

13 Barry Manilow

14 The Stadium of Light in Sunderland

15 Marks & Spencer

16 2006

17 "Like coming home"

18 The Pussycat Dolls

19 Manchester

20 Over 40 million (and counting!)

Picture credits